Industry of Brief Distraction

Laurie Saurborn Young

Distributed by University Press of New England
Hanover and London

Saturnalia Books
105 Woodside Rd.
Ardmore, PA 19003
info@saturnaliabooks.com

ISBN: 978-0-9915454-4-5
Library of Congress Control Number: 2014949482

Book Design by Saturnalia Books
Printing by Westcan Printing Group, Canada

Cover Art: *Asymptote* by Laurie Saurborn Young

Author Photo: Patti James

Distributed by:
University Press of New England
1 Court Street
Lebanon, NH 03766
800-421-1561

The author gratefully acknowledges the editors of the following publications, in which versions of these poems first appeared:

jubilat: "Drone"

Banango Street: "Abortion," "Talking into My Hat," and "Upon Learning of the Word Everlasting"

The American Reader: "In Answer" and "Pretty Girls Are Everywhere"

Better: Culture & Lit: sections of "Various Generations of Plastic Horses"

Columbia Poetry Review: "Sunday Morning"

iO: A Journal of New American Poetry: "Collage of My Best Intentions"

Phantom Limb: "Eudaimonia in Amherst, MA"

Jellyfish Magazine: "After Odysseus Says She's Beautiful"

The Collagist: "Draught"

Forklift, Ohio: "Patriot" (pp. 15 & 44)

The "Patriot" poems were published together in a chapbook of the same name (Forklift, Ink., 2013).

Special thanks to Justin Bigos, Sarah Blake, Laurie Filipelli, Carrie Fountain, Matt Hart, H. L. Hix, Henry Israeli, Patti James, Barbara Ras, Cara Zimmer, and as always, to Dean.

Table of Contents

★

★

for Melissa

all this

Under the untroubled gaze of distant planets

And lesser stars.

~ Kay Boyle

Patriot

Line of thunderstorms on the weather map.
This is America, & so the body, hand-sewn, is over there.
And so at dawn the Carolina water tower is a peach
Rising like the moon's ass.
Finite town, rusted trailer, time-bleached house.
How many foxes did we take under our wheels?
She turns her head and rests her cheek but not completely on his shoulder.
On to Tennessee & the Mouse Ear is a strip
Club where we will not have coffee, not cup a dancer's
Breast before she slaps our hands away.
Where shuttered factories mirror distribution's decline.
Last I saw my ex's mom before she lost to lung
Cancer, we ate at the Shoney's in Brevard,
Back when you could strike up inside & back
When the Biorhythm machine still
Spit out our eternal rhymes.
This horizon fills with Neruda's yellow light.
Since he is tall enough and so she can do her leaning against,
This is America.
So is drinking pale champagne and pouring
Three-fifths of the bottle down the drain.
On to the rest area, tampon in one hand, metal dog bowl in the other.
Line of voters turned away.

Upon Learning of the Word Everlasting

Chinese elms, they laugh. Auburn

cat on the sofa, he smiles too.
What else to say of a broken

binding or a rabbit bounding
back at dawn? Planets converge

but oh yea they falleth apart in great
haste. Tilting windmills stand

giant in my kitchen. I stop kissing
strangers but breathing is escape

so I swim four times a week. Dogs
don't feel this guilty watching prayer

wheels spin in Bhutan. It is inquired
how we spend our days & well

we pass them in their counting.
Sister bright, she wakes in a country

nearing this, among native
plovers faintly heard. A lover

asleep, a cat's paw alighting
on her arm. A heart somewhere

coming closer than it should.
Setting a willow afire I recall who

we are, yard and air one listing
satellite. An old blonde dog

lifted up the steps. And yea verily
we cannot contain our celebration!

Primary industries

Of my great-grandfathers, one spoke

Pentecostic; the other, old German.
Oh how I have worked in brick

        to make of me one further.

In the bath I recite Longfellow's

lost youth, grass and cloud still
visible. Sunlight melts through

window glass, but I am ignoring
the new world for this.

        Meanwhile, cicadas

pull off blistered shells & ride out.

Collage of My Best Intentions

Might as well care, with
nothing left to turn

over in the hands near
midnight or morning.

Green parrots are simply
puppets in the trees,

juggling coals. Nail

holes unveil ten tiny
ports into an ocean.

So I paint the air over my eyes
salt and azure, one

more lonely metropolitan.

Just as time is a dolphin
swimming backward,

I am a pair of somersaulting
arms minus a body.

Culture is a construct,
copper running under

ground an atomic

miracle. Windbreaker
blue on my old man who

stalks up the street.
Who trips over the tangled

hair of a friend who lies
asleep outside in dreams.

In the form of a question:

I paint red cowboy
boots on my feet.

I press heel prints into my palms.

I feed the cat next door
until it says my name.

Don't pass me a cigarette—
I have stopped pretending

to hang dresses in the tree.

Little do we know how laughter
speaks in another's head,

that grey bouquet of shadow.

Vault like a gazelle I will,

outward over water until
I turn into breath. Until I

fall in love with mortar &

climb into a bag of peaches.
Oh, lonely metropolitan,

here you are, drawing off
topography's veil.

Draping it over my face

as we drive along a gentle
border of the sea.

Modern Political Thought

Does not taste the heart chakra's grass-green.

Recalls a friend who lived in the Valley until she blew away.

Squats on earth, fighting among virgin scholars.

Believes erratum when it says my birth is *That of bad timing.*

In the band plays xylophone, French horn, a long
        stringed instrument.

Dahlia-shaped, does burst forth & harbor no great plan.

Notes our jump from cloud & use of lake as trampoline.

Listens to the drum and growl of low animals.

It is *poros* as the Greeks say while traveling

& forevermore blue eyes we do not blink in answer to.

To whom we say, *Remember the way drinking water tastes at home.*

Does not know flight is our foot mantra
        or know the warm streets, umbrella blocking the sun.

Launches above the minds of daughters erupting in air.

Akin to the way sex wavers as light on moving grass.

Lives in an airstream trailer until aluminum
        grows erratic.

Surrounds the spot where hurt shut the spiny doors.

Graphein the Greeks say: where democracy arrayed its fine hats.

Eudaimonia in Amherst, MA

Clever radish: a moon's
red slips behind cloud.

Sparrows fly from ripe
apples. A foot hovers.

Is it marbles in milk
or one searchlight under

water? Incremental farmers
billow along a horizon

wide as an accordion.
A dart in each corner

pulls the four walls in.

Patriot

This is America and alone in a New
England parking lot I look up to five fighter
Planes roaring low in a blue sky and for once everyone
Spills out of the Tire Barn and stares up, too.
On the bed an torn quilt she saved from an early marriage.
On the table I leave the bittersweet vine
For it would rattle apart by Kentucky.
Sitting in the claw-footed tub, morning of her first:
Why not? though she knew.
Forever men taking a break with grease
Under their nails is America.
Is the closed-captioned words *You little*
Bitch on the gym TV and is the dull
Line of women on treadmills
Running steady toward the phrase.
Appalachia to the left, he was manic and said he knew
All he would ever have were girls.
What level of hell, to be the great white
Shark swimming in an aquarium
Tank in the middle of the Midwest?
Just wed they made their way to a patch of lava
Glowing in porous and blackout rocks.
Undecided is refusing to know who it is you inhabit.

Patriot

Emergency room nurses debating
Glocks versus .22s while my husband cannot
Breathe again is America.
Is the boy next door, hitting himself in the head with a stick.
Prometheus, are you seeing this?
No fix, just day-to-day.
Smoky wall, smudged glass, a bite of lemon peel.
Thicket of economy, I want more.
This is America and I will not dance at the country
Club, I will run into the fields & kiss a farmer
Who once cut tobacco in the Piedmont heat.
Somewhere I am sixteen and some-
How I am failing my driver's
Test because I cannot back up for twenty
Feet in a straight line.
Demi-plié, toe shoes on a dusty stage.
My ex was a cheerleader and therefore
On he remarked to great acclaim.
No answers in the clouds, the clouds
Never answer because an answer is not the point.
Blue woman in the painting, her mind not tacked down.
This is America and I am still waiting to be taken
Out of context.

Various Generations of Plastic Horses

1.

Predictable, this distaste for blue
folkloric dress. In our asleep

dreams, we sing all the racers
down. In awake dreams: orgasm.

Quivering knot of lace. As the sun
slips, no one marks you more than I.

Polymer legs net what they can.
Audiences debate the difference

between *cloud* and *could*. Amorphous,
horses canter forth. They know

extinction holds incalculable joy.

2.

Skim fifty pages of a soundless
sleep. Dust flies up from plucked

strings. Rumple-headed, twenty-
five years later, finding my crush

on Han Solo means I would rather
be Indiana Jones. Thinned taut,

this sky. Turns out the membrane
between here & there effervesces.

Suddenly, a plastic bay on the step.

So let me ask you how you are.
Let me listen when you answer.

3.

All we can do, bedding down in dry
leaves. In awake dreams, it's temporal.

In asleep dreams, the clannish night
drones on. Gravity motions: sit here.

Impossible to shake, plastic horses.
Who say we will lose our loves

drastically, and again, even while

warm in this bright-armed world.
Sleeping. Human. It makes small

difference. What more can a trumpet
shout to the scattering sky?

4.

All a breathing horse knows of reason,
accommodation and of lack would

fill a plastic horse. How is it that people
we love will not return home?

Brittle angels, the carts go less.

Dawn is the mask of a sleepy, pointed
bird. Or the mysterious and gradual

disappearance of candle from thin
wick. There are too many of us here.

Yet we land in trees and climb down.
Yet pliant, the fresher go forth.

5.

Muchacha en la ventana—Dalí's
woman at the window. Turn each

year into the form of a plastic horse.

Branches fall and burst into apple.
Wherein swaddled old days? Wherein

bright dippers, drought holding
fast? Devising the word happitude,

we mean to commit it to memory.
What is it to lose people until we

are lost ourselves & so, absolved?
See the sun, a camphor disc.

6.

Scattered like confetti of fire: ruddy

crepe myrtle and all Éluard
said, or didn't, about a woman

I will fall in love with. Who in time
will depart with a Polish chanteuse.

Melancholy face, bandit of the high
terracotta style. Or amethysts now

petals in our teeth. A blanket draped
over the horse's sweated back.

Mouth, how happy in the corn-
flower nest between your legs.

7.

Bees deep drunk in paper-
white & hyacinth. Waves

spilling out, pulling back. Nerve-

racking, all this running
about with a seedling

tucked between coniferous
hands. In asleep dreams, we fly.

In our galloping dream, house-
holds absolved of their salt.

Oscillation of red barns.
Hoof picks, ringing the bells.

8.

Memorize the Western proverb:
Bully love will take axe to trellis.

What shadows trees make of them-
selves! Bare nasturtiums.

Allotted time, here & there.

A lullaby of five cruel lines
about the cut of that horse's gait.

Let the child become, even
if you never meet. Mothers cart

black saddles back & forth as milk-
weed seeds drift into the flame.

9.

Begat the estate, begat the mute mouth
rhymed with Richter's blonde floating

down the stairs. Attend to the reins
in her hand. Herding clouds in fog.

Lemongrass one night, meadow-
foam the next! Brighter the moon,

darker the lake! Half-headed light—

babies we would bear then leave behind.
Language is another word for transition.

Fields full of grain. Soft velvet noses.
Electric blue horse in the plane tree.

10.

In the dream, I am Robert Redford
sitting in a clear-watered lake. One

horseshoe on the bottom indicates
we reign in the Age of Metals.

Regret, inverting itself. How else
goes the old verse? *The bit*

I throw to you is the boot you may
toss back. Over night seas,

horses reconfigure our plans.

In the field a house is constructed
to stand before another house.

Secondary industries

So at the market I ask a pretty girl

whom she allows to touch her hair.
Oh beetle! Oh gentle diatribe!

Looking at myself in the freezer
doors I see I should not have

     run so fast to get here,

face wavering over frozen peas.

Nothing for me to tell this girl
in exchange, who would not know

oxygen costs $219 a day.
What I have left is a hand

     against cold glass;

several great-grandmothers who

would not know my name.

Patriot

Today I kiss a woman and she turns to salt.
This is America and Morrissey shouts, *The royal*
Family is a dictatorship! & forgive me I want to drop
Him in Hungary, 1942, the place and time
The father of a childhood friend
Escaped in his childhood.
Mother in the airplane aisle, rocking your son:
I love you without envy yet still reaching
Outward and away from one another we persist.
As if by omission as if Hemingway's
Hadley had neither face nor tears.
People everywhere are just people everywhere
Tearing down what they replenish.
Chekhov's chemist mostly sleeping through it all.
Meanwhile a wave grows & an old Japanese couple
Lifts their dog into their arms.
This is America and I am still perming my hair,
Still on the back of a battered
Four-wheeler, still shrieking as we buck
Up a hill. So we never fucked.
So what. Is it rude to admit one's limits?
Engaged on Mt. Katahdin she refused to hike the ridge.
America is water approaching, is the camera cutting away.

Patriot

From where we stand, this is America.
Not-here, matter, and spirit are the three
States we shuffle through. Brick
Church and stoned-at-school are the solid ones.
So shout to the immobilized sky: *Lolita's in my car!*
So if married and trailed by a private
Eye there are three actions to avoid:
Do not run a stoplight.
Do not speed to any man's house and drop a bottle of rich
Red wine on the concrete drive.
Tail knocked off until the tail was further off.
From where they stood in the kitchen she could taste the bed.
Skyline Drive, spine of mountains: fake being lost.
A woman died so with an axe he broke
Down the wheelchairs she made.
Closed are the X-ray film plant & center for appliance
Distribution. Fallen are so many dead
Deer along the American highways.
Telephone poles, their postures long
Outdated. In mind only, yet
Determined, he took her against waterfall,
Sheet of film, hard through a line of voters
Occupied with turning away.

Patriot

Guessing a medical term for *meaningless* is America.

Mastiff eating 2x4s, as a child unafraid I pet you.

The marriage is in the house, he said.

Yet somewhere she is eighteen and next

Morning in cold Wyoming he rides out to the paddock,

Lets all the horses free to fend in winter.

The chemist's wife watches from the window.

Her ribcage upside down a butterfly.

This is America and reaching El Paso the sky turns

Silver, the earth blurs and rises.

Where is it we are?

Android David says, *I was designed like this because you*

People are more comfortable

Interacting with your own kind.

Still throwing women in the water to see *if* is America.

Homemade yogurt, cherries red in peach jam.

I changed the locks, he said.

Remarks are not literature, Stein said

By the pond where my sister and I fed summer

Ducks stale white bread, where we ran

From the tall honking goose.

Someone always in the process of taking over

With orange beak angled wide is America.

Drone

Trucks on the road

haul pieces of a factory

to the factory.

Past grey-white

sails on an ice

blue bay.

Past a dog wearing

her face all day.

With a linen

towel of Tang-bright

fish I dry

three singing bowls

thinking of among

other things, the loss of three

million trees over

last summer's vacation.

Reclining girl on the side-

walk thinks: sky.

Thinks if men are kings

here, a rose is a rose is a rose

is Arose Street, which we cross.

Last night I danced

with the blonde while

around us you loped

fake-barking at the stars.

Soft & august, the cool

moon spilling down

onto a neighbor's drive.

Meanwhile, women bear

men who send

trucks on roads to haul

pieces of a factory to the factory

until July is too

cold for wisteria to bloom.

Dumbass in sunglasses

interviews a survivor

says I hear you

made a quick recovery.

She sighs

deeply, a door

swings open.

Into paper

mills and plastics.

Into fertilizers, scenting the breeze.

Men are kings here so

explain how teak

weathers until it glows.

So say how rock

oil and whale

were first hunted

lit and burned.

Six months since last

I touched the woman

who drove the truck

wearing a muddy

ribbon in her hair.

Marigolds in summer

are small faces

echoing fire.

Among people, the girl

shot in her head by men

hidden among

other men. Having lost

her dog she becomes

invisible to dogs.

An owl flies into

my mouth, my hands

fly into the sun.

Chain of time, send

word of the next

exception, bomber, rose.

Speak of the remote

travesty of white

caps. Of yellow

helicopters in the sky.

Patriot

Collarbone broken & then I am pushed
Hard off the boat. This is America.
If entry is not desired, take that door away.
You want to say I deserved it
Which is often what people think
When force is brought against a woman's
Smaller frame. Diplomatic, I desire little
Cows in a range of shapes:
Miniature but representative
Lowing in a field outside Hershey, PA.
Faint purple smudges under his dark eyes.
Sound of a dog's feet in the grass.
This is Humbert, taping a note to Rita's belly.
Bioluminescence of the highway at night,
What is America?
Four years later she listens to the mixtape
In the parking lot at Snuffer's Restaurant and Bar:
Girl, don't go away mad. Girl, just go away.
Inside I pin my hair up & the bartender
Turns & says to my boyfriend, *Oh, now I see.*
Texas in winter is a silver caul stretched
Thin and babies born into not enough
Jobs not enough medicine not enough water.

Patriot

Whose child sank in the muddy pond is America.

Not under the bed with the cat.

Not outside in pines with the owls.

At fourteen my cousin smiles: two hundred

Beer cans line his bedroom wall

On his farm where I first hear a horse piss.

Do you mean we came from marrow?

From within the intercostals or did we tear them apart.

Hiking in the Petrified Forest, my sister and I laugh

When expecting upright trees we find

Toppled stones baking in gold heat is America.

Snowflake, temple wall, a stance

Assumed in prayer, or not.

To begin with it is always the beginning.

In joy I fall over. In falling over in joy do I stand up.

How she wanted to kiss him but drank

Three glasses of tepid water instead.

Float or drown? Maybe it was a mistake,

Giving their daughter a name.

Red rocks of Arizona one house in the distance

Leave it alone.

This is America, roughshod & a habit

Sometimes I would wish to break.

Patriot

America is missile seeking same.
Is domesticated wolf just along for the ride.
Spastic ash and monopolies, what polis
Is this where we spend ourselves to debt?
Drug dealer at the stoplight, tattooed
In pen ink. It's the Seventies,
Farrah's winged & it's impossible to feed a family
On what remains in the wide and yet so fields.
Secret code, broken microscope, dog very
Present in her gone.
There are many ways to be asleep.
To be a blue bird
Unfolding in our each & bandaged eyes.
Tolerant spirits, we tire of raising you
Among the swamp'd and mangrove'd waters.
Among sirens lifting into coyotes' cries.
Never his face she dismayed but the over-
Wrought landscapes of Delaware.
But cleaning the shower in grief at 5am.
What else but Eastern daffodils, but white
Mountain laurels in wet spring?
But the conversion of America into a stained
Glass bank, thick with light?

Tertiary industries

One who might wash the wounds.
Who might carve radishes in-

to pale flower—

who would not see dawn burst into fog.
Steps lead up or down for a while,

then are taken away. Just
forms in space, the riddle turns out.

       How's that? the great-grandfathers

ask—but they never mean to hear
my reply. When the screen

falls off the window I think
it will make me easier to find.

                But then I worry moonlight

might drag me away.

Pretty Girls Are Everywhere

Apple-faced love, where is your light
delay? Self is the brain's exhaust.
Nabokov drove through Texas, singing—

Thieves & watchtowers! Fuck them all!
And what of the sky's distraction,
its building of clouds? And what of my

sweat falling in lost & tender
stars? Tiny Tim succumbs to heart
failure and a detective is hot

on the trail of our bottles. Strong
as trances we do not desist, our dog
now spring's Armageddon. Debating

silver lining, we chant *metallic cloud*
until crows are born with blue
eyes. *Opera of flesh, wherein a beginning?*

I think to ask the sandwich girl.
This week we watch *The Fox*
& the Hound with a blossomed

                                        grey sense of foreboding.
                                Yes auburned hair of some trees!
                                Yes skylights filled with loblolly

pines! Give us lavender drunk
down in Banyuls wine. A plum
tree, blooming fast. Maybe Plato's

lost loves, converted to bombs?
I ask a girl what it means & she says
Angel with a fuse in his mouth. She

says *Plastic fables and manes.* When
she is drunk I watch *Ancient Aliens,*
our ocean rising from its knees.

After Odysseus Says She's Beautiful

Beside goats with urine-soaked beards.
Despite an Amish doll my sister

pulls from the closet shelf.
We map the Pleiades & find

little comfort from distant groupings.

At night we imagine blue dust
over everything: our bed, the mirrors.

The rowboats at dawn.

With scant water we form a year
from our cells dusting this floor.

As eyes, so mouth. Singing, an ex-

wife's red hair in the drain.

Night spills nebulae over our heads.
Our hands quickly become

flocks of fragile silver birds.

Faceless clocks falling
down a well.

Or a handful of crickets
hoping to follow us home.

My sister keeps the chart of tarnished

lockets while souls go
about their crossings.

Go about their returns.

Proto-industries

Tonight at the hospital I see
another girl wearing green

pajamas, yellow mask pulled
over half her southward face.

Pacing to weave

       sustenance, up or

down those stairs.

I have slept soundly in forty-
nine states and know it is okay

     to be broken and waiting

for someone to call your name.
Three floors up, you sleep.

This girl is surely

       taller in my mind, blonder

than wheat in wildfire.

Patriot

Great-grandfather, Free Will preacher who
Had a stroke & could not speak, you
Are and were America, too.
Population booming we are not unique,
Everyone breathing in place.
Again she sweeps the steps, again the oak
Leaves drift back as screens shift in their frames.
Smell of circus elephants in the sky,
Two men sit at a table & discuss how
Much they like to cry.
Off with their heads!
Sappho, then silence for many years.
We are mammals, mammals are animals
So consciousness is a trait of animals
In the hospital at midnight or noon.
Is a junco flying dark-eyed from the clouds.
Is temple, parlor, pew.
She broke into the house to find the marriage
And she saw what Hemingway struck
Were his tears, spilling out.
Were meditations & socks lost under the couch.
Over here we do it slower keep the head,
Put a faulty line into the arm is America.

Patriot

Smiles on wet glass is America, families
Holding hats in their hands.
Oracle notwithstanding,
Surely not all the munchkins
Tried to peek up Dorothy's dress?
Not Algiers, not Sycorax,
But Central Station where a man waits
In his jacket soon dropped to a hotel room floor.
Our stomachs sing like blue whales.
Our hands clap under rest stop dryers.
Who lives beneath a true tin roof is America.
Who passes the bottle of whiskey around
In a trailer by Hood River is me.
Somewhere it is 1930 & my aunt is the first
Woman to wear pants in Holmes County.
Unknown to you does not mean out of the ordinary,
She said, re-lacing her boots.
Maple leaves drift on the Hudson's steel shine.
Stop casting back, we have enough women
Existing only in degree of nymph.
Blue topaz burned the earrings in his hand.
Paternal riot is America.
Hooves of starving horses are America, too.

Draught

Much happens every day until it disappears.

I dream I am the sound of a hand
ringing a bell. *Surely the people is grass*

Isaiah wrote, but every-
one thought it a joke.

No stars staring out the window—
just desert-locked me.

Who cannot tell if rain sinks
ecstatic or laments drawing

down the rabbit's nose.

Much happens every
day and then it disappears.

Poor laugh, poor
man. All week the leaves

pray to a deciduous
god until I dream

I am the sound of a bell

ringing a bell.

Talking into My Hat

What could happen if clouds
undressed themselves at night

instead of knocking on our door,

       begging *unlace, untie?*

My dog is blind and most
stars as well, so we can get

away with anything. With a rust
red hawk perching

       on the wire—though might it fall
apart in my hands?

We will become exactly
what we'll become, by which

I mean a woman carries
       persimmons to a distant morning

market. By which I mean I pull my hat

over my face to spend time among
any other thought. Rumor

indicates this train moves

exactly as it should, toward some
god of Carthage.

Or is it carnage? I forget.

Days of the week, their burnt
edges and smells—

I don't forget them. Where is the little

man who unicycles my heart?
I have never seen a picture of my

self as a child but I am not

thinking of our souls at all.

Abortion

No linear blessing, only a pink
Paper umbrella, tanked lobsters

Waving wide claws and the friend
Who stops calling. A father who says

Green-black grackles in the yard
Tell him to walk back inside.

Stubbornly I focus, though some
Force persists in twisting

This lens. Insists on removing
My country. Now what flag, if any,

May I fly? As a child I signaled
Back to the lobsters; I kept trinkets

Gracing adult drinks in my top
Dresser drawer. No matter how fast

You rake, oak leaves still float down.
No matter what you believe, a call

Rings out again. After all this,
What world is it where a bird

Tells a man to go and he does?

Patriot

Fighting in a night-damp field is America,
Her shirt unbuttoned one too far.
Nothing static within the lit windows I stare
Into at night while walking the dog & wishing
Winter might remain for just a season more.
Why not everything?
Maybe the blue flame is what Strauss
Meant, doubt something swept along the floor.
Furnace groaning she sat on the cellar steps,
Listened to his wrench bite at cold pipes.
Somewhere I am eighteen and somewhere I still
Plan to get drunk & pass out, then awake
Nearly twenty years later to find
You still means *Men in the audience.*
Adirondack chairs wait in dark fields.
You strangers who wish me harm yet invite me
With greatest chivalry into your cars:
Often I think of you speeding off.
Of the variolations of Abigail Adams.
Of a river otter diving in Port Townsend Bay.
Of Seymour side-stroking out to the waves
& kissing a small girl's sun-salted
Foot until it is America, too.

Quaternary industries

Birdbath, apron, tire chains in snow:
all hoping for a line of *unto*.

A line of *begat*.

Cap lifted, sweat on brow,
I think of another girl

who tried to overdose on aspirin.

Of how we are all the woman
washing her face in the stream.

Sick with the flu
I put on a new perfume,

       hoping in slight

alteration to find one answer.
But I become violet, my soup

stays violet, the tables & sky

saturated as well. Once
I had no tone or scent—

I had no form for illness—

as before my great-grandmothers

         rose a body of water.

In Answer

Because the world goes

on being gorgeous,

I will not complain

about a stray cat crying on the front
porch; about summer heat

warming water in the pipes.

At lunch I order the Homewrecker
but only because I am hungry

and platonic.

There are things I wish for, such

as a red circle

skirt. But I don't feel like going
so far out of my way.

Because it is not one

life that I look back upon,

the emergency is over and I may

collect samples again.

      I can smell like oranges

              while grackles explode

from our names into the sky.

Sunday Morning

As instructed, I erase my German
childhood. Omit my mother's tiny

stamping foot. My father's vest
I catch in a great and laughing

fire! Cut across chickens & there
spring feathers. Cut across our lawn

& there waits the street. For weeks
I take the days two at a time.

Hawks turn to flower as my sister
sends tutor after tutor away.

Patriot

Mostly Americans, my friends are getting married
Again so I forswear the birds this time.
But now I want a house along Blue Ribbon Avenue,
Where sloths are elastic because they feel safe.
Standing in one room they gauge the bed in another room.
Everyone's wiser than me: Yeah, I get it.
Still, down the long hall they did not walk.
So sing along the drive: *This is America*
Irreplaceable and yet
Unnecessary and yet loved.
Meanwhile, Fate is a city in Texas.
Far away those homes next to homes of men, yelling.
Season of black powder, of wrenches rusting in the rain.
But is it true, that sign along the Arkansas
Highway: *I love and miss you.*
But is this America, still debating
Whether as a woman, whether I am worth.
Our roads, imported from Spain.
Our telephone call, nearing ancient.
Within a room constructed of shut doors he reads
Pages back to her, his back to her.
Lines disintegrate. It is ever so late.
After she voted, she took her body, she took it back home.

Notes

1. The epigraph is from Kay Boyle's poem, "After the Earth Quaked."
2. "Collage of My Best Intentions": "Lonely Metropolitan" is a photograph by Herbert Bayer.
3. "Patriot" (pp. 15 & 32) contains quotes from the movie, *Prometheus*.
4. "Various Generations of Plastic Horses" (p. 24) refers to Gerhard Richter's photograph, *Ema (Nude Descending a Staircase)*.
5. "Patriot" (p. 32): "Remarks are not literature" quoted from Gertrude Stein's *The Autobiography of Alice B. Toklas*.
6. "Drone": "Men are kings here" quoted from Lt. Colonel Malalai Kakar, an Afghani policewoman killed by the Taliban, in 2008. The poem also refers to the ordeal of Malala Yousafzai, a Pakistani student and activist attacked by Taliban militants in 2012.
7. "Drone": "A rose is a rose is a rose is a rose" quoted from Gertrude Stein's *Sacred Emily*.
8. "Patriot" (p. 44): "Girl, don't go away mad. Girl, just go away" quoted from Mötley Crüe's "Don't Go Away Mad (Just Go Away)."
9. "Pretty Girls Are Everywhere": Stanza two references Bob Dylan's "All Along the Watchtower."
10. "Draught" quotes Isaiah 40:7 (King James Bible): "The grass withereth, the flower fadeth: because the spirit of the LORD bloweth upon it: surely the people *is* grass."
11. "In Answer": "It is not one life that I look back upon" quoted from Virginia Woolf's *The Waves*.